The Rosary for Episcopalians/ Anglicans

SECOND REVISED EDITION

ISBN-13: 978-1-58790-055-6
ISBN 10: 1-58790-055-6

A Co-Publication of

REGENT PRESS
2747 Regent Street
Berkeley, CA 94705
regentpress@mindspring.com
www.regentpress.net
and
INCARNATION PRIORY PRESS
c/o MOUNT CALVARY
  Monastery and Retreat House
P.O. Box 1296
Santa Barbara, CA 93102-1296
Mtcalvary1@aol.com
www.mount-cavalry.org

Copyright © 1992, 2003 by the Order of the Holy Cross. All rights reserved.
First edition 1992. Second edition 2003. Printed in the United States of America.

The Mysteries of Christ, of the Resurrection, and of Sacramental Life on
pages 13-15 are quoted from *Praying by Hand: Rediscovering the Rosary as a Way of
Prayer, by* M. Basil Pennington, o.c.s.o., (New York: Harper-Collins), and are
reprinted by permission.

The Scriptural passages in the Appendix are quoted from the *New Revised
Standard Version of the Bible,* copyright © 1989, Division of Christian Education
of the National Council of Churches of Christ in the United States of America.
Used by permission. All rights reserved.

Third Printing   2011
Fourth Printing 2013

The Rosary for Episcopalians/Anglicans

WHY PRAY? Because Jesus said to. This is our response to God for the gift of God's life in us begun with our Baptism. All of our prayers are begun in the Spirit, continue through the Son, to the Father. And so all our prayerful response to God is caught up in the life of the Trinity. Our response is of two kinds: one is prayer joined with others, and this is corporate prayer; and the second is private prayer. In this second response, there are many forms, and the one I would like to present to you comes from the pre-Reformation spiritual treasury of the Church. It is the Rosary.

Rosaries in many forms, with different numbers of beads, are found in all the major religions of the world. From the earliest times, people have used a string of knots in a cord, or beads on a string, for keeping count of prayers offered to God. In records of the lives of the desert dwellers of the Christian tradition, they carried a set number of pebbles, which were then discarded as the prayer was said. John Cassian, writing of them in the Fourth Century, stated that there were two forms of private prayer in the desert: (1) a set number of prayers, or (2) a set time of prayer, with the prayers themselves being at random. As time passed, the pocketful of pebbles to keep count of a set number of prayers evolved into a string with a set number of beads on it. It could be used over and over again, and became a convenient tool for the prayer life of the desert. Thus began the evolution of the Rosary in both Eastern and Western Christianity.

What is the present form of the Christian Rosary? Looking through *The Book of Common Praise (Revised 1938): Being the Hymn Book of the Church of England in Canada*, on page 786 we find Katherine Hankey's hymn, written in 1868, the familiar refrain being:

> I love to tell the story;
> 'Twill be my theme in glory

> To tell the old, old story
> Of Jesus and his love.

What better description of the Rosary? It is the story of our salvation seen in the life of Jesus Christ. In the past, this was done in three sets of five Mysteries, each Mystery being a portion of Scripture as a basis of meditation on the Life of Christ. Today, this is done in four sets of five Mysteries.

The first set is called the *Joyful Mysteries,* which are as follows:
1. The Annunciation *Luke* 1:26–38[1]
2. The Visitation *Luke* 1:39–56
3. The Nativity *Matt.* 1:18–2:12, *Luke* 2:1–20
4. The Presentation *Luke* 2:22–35
5. The Finding in the Temple *Luke* 2:41–52

The second set, added by Pope John Paul II in 2002, is called the *Luminous Mysteries,* which are as follows:
1. The Baptism of Jesus in the Jordan *Matt.* 3:13–17, *Mark* 1:9–11, *Luke* 3:21–22, *John* 1:29–34
2. The Wedding at Cana *John* 2:1–11
3. The Preaching of the Coming of the Kingdom of God
   (A) *Matt.* 4:12–17 *&* 23–25, *Mark* 1:14–15, *Luke* 4:14–21
   (B) *Matt.* 9:2–8, *Mark* 2:3–12, *Luke* 5:18–26
   (C) *Matt.* 26:6–13, *Mark* 14:3–9, *Luke* 7:36–50, *John* 12:1–8
4. The Transfiguration *Matt.* 17:1–8, *Mark* 9:2–8, *Luke* 9:28–35
5. The Institution of the Eucharist *Matt.* 26:17–29, *Mark* 14:12–25, *Luke* 22:7–20, *I Cor.* 11:23–26

The third set of mysteries puts the Cross in the center of our prayer life, as it was central in Christ's life. This set is called the *Sorrowful Mysteries,* and they are as follows:
1. The Agony in the Garden *Matt.* 26:36–46, *Mark* 14:32–42, *Luke* 22:39–46
2. The Scourging *Matt.* 27:15–26, *Mark* 15:6–15, *Luke* 23:13–24, *John* 18:38*b*–19:1
3. The Crowning with Thorns *Matt.* 27:27–31*a*, *Mark* 15:16–20*a*, *John* 19:2–3
4. The Bearing of the Cross *Matt.* 27:31*b*–32, *Mark* 15:20*b*–21, *Luke* 23:26–32, *John* 19:16–17

---
[1] The texts of the Bible passages cited here are given in the Appendix

5. The Crucifixion *Matt.* 27:33–50, *Mark* 15:22–37, *Luke* 23:33–46, *John* 19:18–30

The fourth set is the *Glorious Mysteries,* which are as follows:
   1. The Resurrection *Matt.* 28:1–10, *Mark* 16:1–8, *Luke* 24:1–12, *John* 20:1–18
   2. The Ascension *Mark* 16:19–20, *Luke* 24:50–53, *Acts* 1:6–11
   3. The Coming of the Holy Spirit at Pentecost *Acts* 2:1–4
   4. The Assumption of the Virgin Mary *Rev.* 12:1
   5. The Coronation of the Virgin Mary *II Tim.* 4:8

The preceding, together with the new Luminous Mysteries, are the traditional forms as found in Western Christianity. These are prayed on a rosary made up of five sets of ten beads called a decade, from the Latin word for ten. The Dominican order made this form of the Rosary popular, as a method of teaching salvation history. It is thus known popularly as the Dominican Rosary.

Praying the Rosary is a deliberately chosen, objective act of prayer on our part, focusing on the saving acts of Jesus as found in the Gospels. This act of prayer is an end in itself, and is offered to God as an act of thanksgiving and loving adoration, for the fullness of God's life in us through Baptism. It is also a way to prepare ourselves for contemplation and silence.

What should I expect? God only knows! Or rather, only God knows. Anything that we experience while in prayer, using the Rosary or not, is a gift from God, if it produces in us the Gifts of the Spirit. Don't cling to the experience, or try to reproduce it. Remember, "Always focus on the giver, never on the gift;" this saying of Dom John Chapman, O.S.B., applies here. To prepare ourselves to experience God in our lives is a holy thing in and of itself, and prayer is part of our working at preparing the garden of our soul, sowing the seed of prayer, and waiting for the gentle rains of God to bring in the harvest. While waiting, we can say the Rosary, and learn our salvation history, and patience. Remember: rhythmic, repetitive prayer is not done for *our* edification or intellectual stimulation, but is done as an act of love, thanksgiving, and praise of God. The focus is on God, not us.

Robert Llewelyn, in *A Doorway to Silence: The Contemplative Use of the Rosary* (Paulist Press, 1986), says on page *x* of his introduction,

> The rosary has been, for many, a way in to silent prayer. The silence of the heart before God is of the essence of the prayer life. It is well for

newcomers to the rosary to understand this. We start with the mind gently enfolded in the words *(or it may be resting in one of the mysteries)* and very properly they are the focus of our attention. After a while that focus is likely to begin to disappear from consciousness, and this is where the beginner may become alarmed. What is happening, however, is that—so long as the intention to pray remains—the heart is being drawn gently into the silence beyond the words. The quality of the silence which may be ours when the words have dropped away completely at the end of the exercise will itself be proof that this process has been taking place. Anyone who is experienced in the use of the rosary will at once understand the significance of what is being said. The newcomer will probably understand only after becoming acquainted with the practice.

Because the Rosary is a form of repetitive prayer, we can relax, feel the beads with our fingers, focus on the current mystery, and slowly repeat the prayer. This is not the vain repetition that Jesus warns us about, but repetitive prayer which is done willfully, with intention, and focused on God. We don't have to prove whether the Rosary "works" or not. It has proved itself over the centuries, and brought countless numbers to holiness in God. Therefore, give yourself to the recitation of the prayer, and let your mind focus on that. At the beginning of each decade, recall the mystery, and then begin the prayer.

What Does the Rosary Look Like?

The Rosary is a grouping of beads arranged in groups of ten, called decades. There are five groups of ten separated by a single bead in between the decades. These are joined by a medal to form a circle. The medal may have a picture of Jesus and Mary on it. It is usually in the form of a triangle, and from the bottom point there is a pendant made up of one bead, then a space, three beads, another space, then a final bead, and a crucifix. This is the form of the five-decade Dominican Rosary.

How Do You Use It?

1. To begin the Rosary, holding the crucifix in your hand, make the sign of the cross. This is done by taking the fingers of your right hand and touching your forehead saying, "In the name of the Father

..." then touching your chest and saying, "... and of the Son ..." then the left shoulder, "... and of the Holy ..." and finally the right shoulder, "... Spirit. Amen." Then, still holding the cross, recite the Apostles' Creed (see pages 7 & 8 for the forms of prayers). This is the creed of our Baptism.

2. Moving up the pendent, holding the first bead above the crucifix, say the OUR FATHER (the Lord's Prayer).

3. Moving up the pendant, say the HAIL MARY on each of the next three beads, for the intention of the increase of the gifts of Faith, Hope, and Charity. On the chain, in the space before the next bead, say the GLORY TO THE FATHER (the *Gloria Patri*).

4. The next bead, right before the medal, is the OUR FATHER bead that begins the first mystery. Holding the bead, recall the mystery you wish to offer, then begin the OUR FATHER.

5. Moving past the medal, start up the right hand side of the circle, gently reciting the HAIL MARY on each of the next ten beads.

6. After the HAIL MARY on the last of the ten beads, say the GLORY TO THE FATHER on the chain.

7. Moving to the bead that begins the next mystery, recall the second mystery in the series, and repeat the recitation as above for the first mystery. Begin with the OUR FATHER, then say ten HAIL MARY's, ending with the GLORY TO THE FATHER.

8. Continue along all the beads until you arrive back at the medal.

9. To end the Rosary, the collect for the Feast of the Annunciation may then be said on the medal.

You have now said the Rosary. As you become more familiar with the handling of the Rosary and the memorizing of the prayers, you will be able to carry it in your pocket, or wake at night, and without turning on the light, take up your Rosary, and by touch, find your way around this familiar form of repetitive prayer.

Rosary Prayers

THE APOSTLES' CREED
I believe in God, the Father almighty,
   creator of heaven and earth.
I believe in Jesus Christ, his only Son, our Lord.
   He was conceived by the power of the Holy Spirit
   and born of the Virgin Mary.

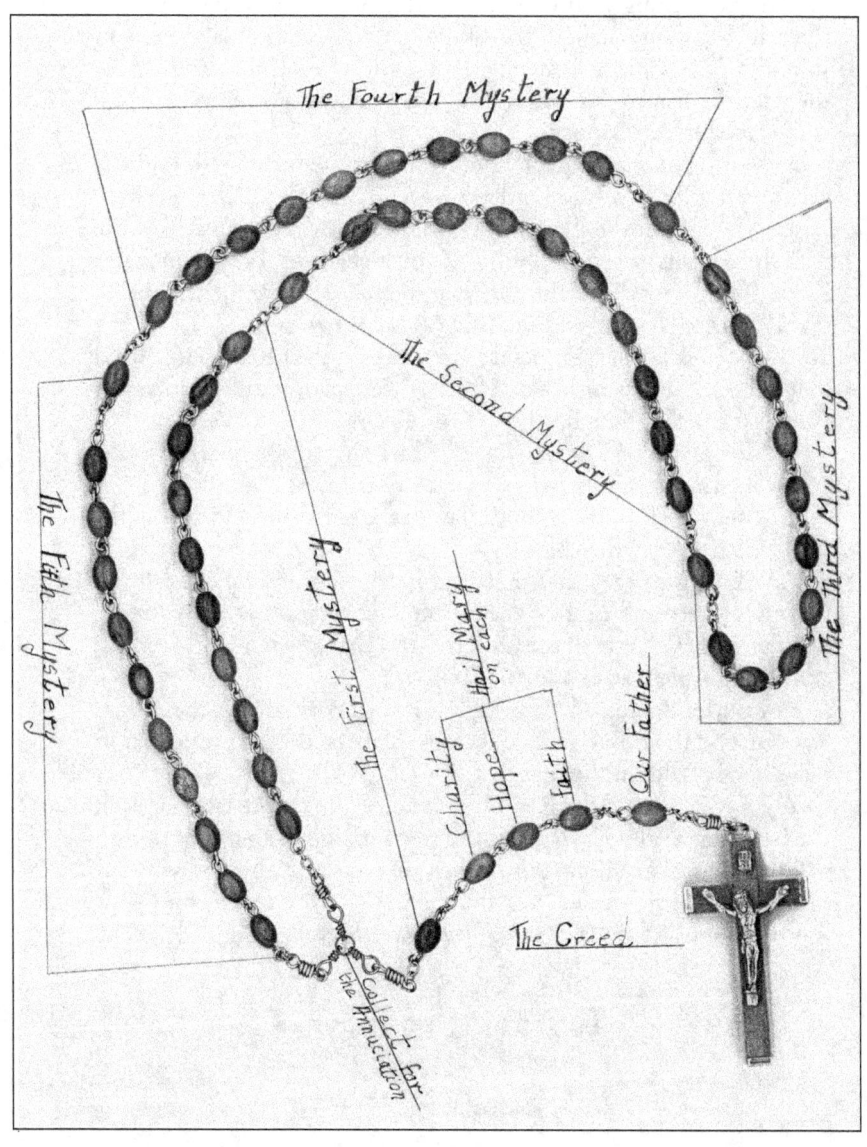

He suffered under Pontius Pilate,
> was crucified, died, and was buried.
He descended to the dead.
On the third day he rose again.
He ascended into heaven,
> and is seated at the right hand of the Father.
He will come again to judge the living and the dead.
I believe in the Holy Spirit,
> the holy catholic Church,
> the communion of saints,
> the forgiveness of sins,
> the resurrection of the body,
> and the ✠ life everlasting. Amen.

Book of Common Prayer, pp. 53–54 & 96

THE OUR FATHER (LORD'S PRAYER)

Our Father in heaven,
> hallowed be your Name,
> your kingdom come,
> your will be done,
>> on earth as in heaven.
Give us today our daily bread.
Forgive us our sins
> as we forgive those who sin against us.
Save us from the time of trial,
> and deliver us from evil.

Book of Common Prayer, pp. 132–3

THE HAIL MARY

Hail Mary, full of grace, the Lord is with you. Blessed are you among women, and blessed is the fruit of your womb, Jesus. * Holy Mary, Mother of God, pray for us sinners, now and at the hour of our death. Amen.

Traditional

The Glory to the Father (*Gloria Patri*)

Glory to the Father, and to the Son, and to the Holy Spirit: * as it was in the beginning, is now, and will be for ever. Amen.

Book of Common Prayer, p. 131

The Collect for the Feast of the Annunciation (March 25)

Pour your grace into our hearts, O Lord, that we who have known the incarnation of your Son Jesus Christ, announced by an angel to the Virgin Mary, may by his cross and passion ✠ be brought to the glory of his resurrection; who lives and reigns with you, in the unity of the Holy Spirit, one God, now and for ever. Amen.

Book of Common Prayer, p. 240

These are the prayers for the recitation of the Rosary. For a corporate recitation, the leader begins the Creed, and all recite it together. The same is true of the recitation of the Our Father. The recitation of the Hail Mary is begun by the leader, and recited up to the asterisk. Then the group responds with all that follows the asterisk. The same is true of the Glory to the Father.

Over the centuries, popular piety has overlaid the rosary with devotional fervor for Mary, the mother of Jesus, the *Theotokos,* meaning the God-bearer (*Book of Common Prayer,* page 864). This definition of Mary's role in our salvation story was translated in Western Christianity into the phrase "Mother of God." This phrase, over the centuries, became attached to two other phrases from the Gospel; namely, "Hail, full of grace, the Lord is with you," from the Annunciation narrative, and "Blessed are you among women, and blessed is the fruit of your womb," from the Visitation narrative. Over time, the name of Mary was added to the first passage, and the name of Jesus was added to the end of the second passage. The request for the prayer of Jesus' Mother, "Holy Mary, Mother of God, pray for us sinners, now and at the hour of our death. Amen," gives us the well known prayer, the Hail Mary:

> Hail Mary, full of grace, the Lord is with you. Blessed are you among women, and blessed is the fruit of your womb, Jesus. Holy Mary, Mother of God, pray for us sinners, now and at the hour of our death. Amen.

What is Mary's role in the story of salvation history as found in the Rosary? Our salvation history began with her reply to Gabriel, God's messenger at the Annunciation. At the Visitation, she sings the *Magnificat,* as she bears the Son of God in her womb. Later at the wedding feast in Cana, she tells the servants, "whatever he tells you to do, do it" (John 2:5). She points to the pouring out of Jesus' life in the Joyful, Luminous, and Sorrowful mysteries, and the exaltation and hope found in the Glorious mysteries. So in effect, she is constantly pointing, not to herself, but to Jesus and his role in our salvation history. It is not by chance that one of her symbols in religious art is the moon, which gets all its radiance from the reflection of the sun.

WHAT ABOUT ASKING MARY to pray for us? Both my parents are dead, but I still pray for them. But because they are in a different relationship with God now, I also ask for their prayers as well. Mary, the first among the saints in heaven, can also be asked to pray for us, just as any who have entered that blessed company can; for all her prayers, like ours and theirs, end, "through Jesus Christ our Lord." He is Mary's Lord as well as ours. So ask!

The preceding prayers are the traditional forms of prayers to be used with the five-decade Rosary. However, there are other forms of prayers that can be used. For instance, in place of the HAIL MARY, there are the following substitutes:

Lord Jesus Christ, Son of the Living God, *
have mercy on me, a sinner.
(This can be shortened, the name of Jesus being the only essential part)

Father, we glorify your name.
(A prayer frequently used by Jesus)

Holy God, Holy and Mighty, Holy Immortal One, *
have mercy upon us.
(Trisagion)

Abba, Father, * I belong to you.

Since the Rosary is part of the spiritual treasury of private prayer, instead of liturgical prayer, it isn't set, and is open to development. There were at one time three hundred mysteries, and the OUR FATHER was the common prayer used for each bead. There are many books that will help you with further use of the Rosary in your daily prayer life, governing when to say which mysteries, and further development of its use in the prayers of intercession and petition. A number of examples of such further development follow. (Since they were created before the Luminous Mysteries were added in 2002, I have left them in their original form, rather than trying to add to them.)

A Rosary of Intercession

The Rosary may be prayed with special intention using the following formula at the beginning of each decade:

By an individual "O Lord, I offer my prayers and meditations of this mystery as an act of intercession for _____."

Corporately "Let us offer our prayers and meditations during this mystery as an act of intercession for _____."

The Joyful Mysteries
1. Those confused or uncertain about their vocations
2. Our families
3. The poor of the world
4. All bishops, priests, and deacons
5. The aged

The Sorrowful Mysteries
1. The lonely
2. The sick and suffering
3. The President and all in authority
4. Those in despair or discouragement
5. Peace in the world

The Glorious Mysteries
1. The faithful departed
2. All lapsed and indifferent Christians
3. The reunion of all Christians
4. An increase in devotion to the Blessed Virgin
5. Those who have no one to pray for them

A Rosary of Thanksgiving

Same act of intention as found above, substituting the words "act of thanksgiving" for "act of intercession."

The Joyful Mysteries
1. The gift of life
2. The love of family and friends

3. The Church
4. Freedom of worship
5. My priests and teachers over the years.

The Sorrowful Mysteries
1. All who remember me in their prayers
2. The good example and influence of others
3. Our country
4. The opportunity to help others
5. Holy Communion

The Glorious Mysteries
1. For my Baptism
2. For the graces of the Sacrament of Reconciliation
3. For my Confirmation
4. For the example and intercession of Our Lady
5. For the Gift of Faith

A Rosary of Personal Spiritual Growth

The Joyful Mysteries
    A. Adore God the Father.
    B. Ask for the theological virtue of Faith with growth in the Intellect through the Gift of being [*left column*] and the Removal of being [*right column*]:

1. trusting	suspicious
2. confident	fearful
3. co-operative	domineering
4. serene	panicky
5. purposeful	aimless

The Sorrowful Mysteries
    A. Adore God the Son.
    B. Ask for the theological virtue of Hope, with growth in the Will through the Gift of being [*left column*] and the Removal of being [*right column*]:

1. hopeful	despondent
2. encouraging	judgmental
3. patient	impatient
4. assertive	powerless
5. creative in use of gifts	self put-down

The Glorious Mysteries

A. Adore God the Holy Spirit.

B. Ask for the theological virtue of Love (Charity) with growth in the Affections (Emotions) through the Gift of being [*left column*] and the Removal of being [*right column*]

1. outgoing   withdrawn
2. forgiving   resentful
3. caring   indifferent
4. eager for life   apathetic
5. thankful   ungrateful

The rosaries of Intercession, Thanksgiving, and Personal Spiritual Growth are all found in *An Ecumenical Scriptural Rosary*, arranged and edited by the Reverend John G. Moser (Havertown, Pennsylvania: Saint Jude Shop, 1979), pages 8–10. The Rosary of Personal Spiritual Growth is from Mrs. Iris Pearce of Saint Francis' Episcopal Church, Dallas, Texas, and is arranged on the basis of her studies in imagistic prayer therapy.

The following mysteries are by M. Basil Pennington, o.c.s.o., and are taken from his book *Praying by Hand: Rediscovering the Rosary as a Way of Prayer* (New York: HarperCollins), pages 108–115:

THE MYSTERIES OF CHRIST

The Hidden Life

1. Jesus' submission to Mary and Joseph *Luke* 2:51–52
2. Jesus working with Joseph as a carpenter *Mark* 6:1–6
3. Jesus within the extended family *Matt.* 13:53–58
4. The death of Joseph
5. Jesus' parting from Mary *Matt.* 12:46–50

Table Talk

1. At Levi's: He came for us sinners *Matt.* 9:9–13
2. At Simon's: Love is what matters *Luke* 7:36–50
3. At Bethany: Different vocations *Luke* 10:38–42
4. Again at Bethany: Jesus wants us to wait on him *John* 12:1–8
5. At the Cenacle: Jesus gives us the Eucharist *John* 13–14

The Healing Mysteries

1. At Peter's *Matt.* 8:14–17
2. The man lowered through the roof by friends *Mark* 2:1–12

3. The man with the withered hand *Mark* 3:1–6
4. The ten lepers *Luke* 17:11–19
5. The blind man at Jericho *Mark* 10:46–52

"I Am": Jesus' Self-Identity
1. "I am the Bread of Life" *John* 6:35
2. "I am the Gate" *John* 10:9
3. "I am the Good Shepherd" *John* 10:14
4. "I am the Way: I am Truth and Life" *John* 14:6
5. "I am the True Vine" *John* 15:1

THE RESURRECTION MYSTERIES

The Foretypes of the Resurrection
1. Elijah raises the widow's only son *I Kings* 17:17–24
2. Elisha raises the son of the Shunamite *II Kings* 4:8–37
3. Jonah comes out of the whale after three days and three nights *Jonah* 2:1–11
4. Jesus raises the son of the widow of Nain *Luke* 7:11–17
5. Jesus raises Lazarus *John* 11:1–44

Jesus' Resurrection
1. On the road to Emmaus *Luke* 24:13–35
2. Easter night *Luke* 24:36–43
3. A week later *John* 20:24–29
4. By the sea *John* 21:1–23
5. On Olivet *Luke* 24:50–53

SACRAMENTAL LIFE

The Sacraments
1. Baptism *Mark* 1:9–11
2. Confirmation *Acts* 2:1–4
3. Eucharist *Luke* 22:19–20
4. Reconciliation *John* 20:19–23
5. Anointing *James* 5:13–18

The Eucharist
1. The manna in the wilderness *Exod.* 16:4–36
2. The wedding feast at Cana *John* 2:1–12
3. The multiplication of the loaves *John* 6:1–15

4. The Last Supper *Mark 14:22–25*
5. The meal at Emmaus *Luke 24:28–32*

Reconciliation
1. "Though your sins are like scarlet they shall be white as snow." *Isa. 1:18*
2. "A broken, contrite heart you never scorn." *Ps. 51:19*
3. "Her sins, many as they are, have been forgiven her, because she has shown such great love." *Luke 7:47*
4. "Neither do I condemn you." *John 8:11*
5. "Father, forgive them; they do not know what they are doing." *Luke 23:34*

Anointing of the Sick
1. Peter's mother-in-law *Matt. 8:14–15*
2. The centurion's servant *Matt. 8:5–13*
3. The leper *Mark 1:40–45*
4. The official from Capernaum *John 4:46–54*
5. The commission *Mark 6:7–13*

Contemplative Mysteries
1. The Alpha and Omega *Rev. 1:8*
2. The Lion of Judah *Rev. 5:5*
3. The Son of Man *Rev. 14:14*
4. The King of Kings *Rev. 17:14*
5. The Morning Star *Rev. 22:16*

As you can see from the examples given, the Rosary has a form that has been set by tradition, and is recommended to be done in this manner in order to learn it by doing. But the Rosary is also open to further development as we discover more of our life in God through the reading of Scripture, our prayer, and God's guidance.

Through our study of Scripture, we can come up with forms for the Rosary, as described in *Methods of Using the Rosary* by Sister Benedicta, O.S.H.: "A nice set of meditations for a five-decade Rosary is on the use of the word *tharseo* 'take heart, or courage.' It is used five times in the Gospels, each time followed by a reason why one can have courage":

1. "Courage, your sins are forgiven." *Matt.* 9:2
2. "Courage, he is calling you." *Mark* 10:49
3. "Courage, your faith has made you well." *Matt.* 9:22
4. "Courage, it is I." *Matt.* 14:27
5. "Courage, I have conquered the world." *John* 16:33

Sometimes our prayer can be developed and our relationship with God enlightened by non-Scriptural sources. While reading the book, *Revelations of Divine Love,* by Julian of Norwich, in the section "Showings," or visions, I was so struck by how Julian describes how God reveals his relationship with us, that I separated it into five mysteries of God's joy.

1. God rejoices that he is our Father.
2. God rejoices that he is our Mother.
3. God rejoices that he is our soul's true Spouse.
4. Christ rejoices that he is our Brother.
5. Jesus rejoices that he is our Savior.

The very fact that God rejoices in us, just as we are, not as we shall be, is cause of great rejoicing on our part, as well as thanksgiving, and adoration!

IF AFTER A TIME the Rosary becomes a daily practice, the following pattern can be useful to provide balance. The *Joyful Mysteries:* Monday and Saturday, Sundays of Advent; the *Luminous Mysteries:* Thursday, Sundays from Epiphany until Lent; the *Sorrowful Mysteries:* Tuesday and Friday, Sundays in Lent; the *Glorious Mysteries:* Wednesday, Sundays from Easter until Advent.

I HOPE THIS LITTLE PAMPHLET will be of help to those who read it, and that you may take up the Rosary and use it when you care to, and make it a part of your spiritual life. My prayer for all of you who read this is that the Rosary, as a form of prayer, may strengthen you, and lead you into the silence of God's Presence, where you may daily increase in his love and in service to others.

Christ is Risen!

—Thomas Schultz, O.H.C.,
Monk/Priest of the Order of the Holy Cross

INCARNATION PRIORY
Berkeley, California
Easter Monday, 1992

Note to the second edition:

SINCE *The Rosary for Episcopalians* was first compiled and printed, the requests for it have been constant. It has filled a need for a form of piety that is alive and well in the Church. It has been eleven years since I was asked by the Grace Cathedral Bookstore in San Francisco to "write something" about the Rosary, as they had nothing by an Episcopalian on the subject. As a result, this pamphlet came into being. Now, with the Apostolic Letter of Pope John Paul II, *Rosarium Virginis Mariae,* and the creation of the set of "Mysteries of Light," the need to update this work became obvious. I hope the insertion of the Luminous Mysteries has been seamless enough not to be distracting.

The change of the title of the work to *The Rosary for Episcopalians/Anglicans* is owing to the request of many who wrote from outside the United States who are members of the worldwide Anglican Communion. Many Anglicans, they pointed out, don't know what an Episcopalian is, since we in the United States are the only ones using the term, and therefore didn't know that the pamphlet was for them. I hope the change will lessen any confusion.

This booklet was produced with the editorial help of Brother Benedict Littlefield, O.H.C., who also designed it and laid it out.

My prayer for all who take up and read remains as above.

—T.S.
Easter Monday, 2003

APPENDIX
TEXTS OF BIBLICAL CITATIONS

For the reader's ease of reference, a selection from the Bible passages cited on pages 2 & 3 is given below. To save space, representative passages have been selected and their virtually identical parallels omitted.

The Joyful Mysteries

1. THE ANNUNCIATION

Luke 1:26–38

In the sixth month the angel Gabriel was sent by God to a town in Galilee called Nazareth, to a virgin engaged to a man whose name was Joseph, of the house of David. The virgin's name was Mary. And he came to her and said, "Greetings favored one! The Lord is with you." But she was much perplexed by his words and pondered what sort of greeting this might be. The angel said to her, "Do not be afraid, Mary, for you have found favor with God. And now, you will conceive in your womb, and bear a son, and you will name him Jesus. He will be great, and will be called the Son of the Most High, and the Lord God will give to him the throne of his ancestor David. He will reign over the house of Jacob forever, and of his kingdom there will be no end." Mary said to the angel, "How can this be, since I am a virgin?" The angel said to her, "The Holy Spirit will come upon you, and the power of the Most High will overshadow you; therefore the child to be born will be holy; he will be called Son of God. And now, your relative Elizabeth in her old age has also conceived a son; and this is the sixth month for her who was said to be barren. For nothing will be impossible with God." Then Mary said, "Here am I, the servant of the Lord; let it be with me according to your word." Then the angel departed from her.

2. The Visitation

Luke 1:39–56

In those days Mary set out and went with haste to a Judæan town in the hill country, where she entered the house of Zechariah and greeted Elizabeth. When Elizabeth heard Mary's greeting, the child leaped in her womb. And Elizabeth was filled with the Holy Spirit and exclaimed with a loud cry, "Blessed are you among women, and blessed is the fruit of your womb. And why has this happened to me, that the mother of my Lord comes to me? For as soon I heard the sound of your greeting, the child in my womb leaped for joy. And blessed is she who believed that there would be a fulfillment of what was spoken to her by the Lord."

And Mary said,
"My soul magnifies the Lord,
    and my spirit rejoices in God my Savior,
for he has looked with favor on the lowliness of his servant.
    Surely from now on all generations will call me blessed;
for the Mighty One has done great things for me,
    and holy is his name.
His mercy is for those who fear him
    from generation to generation.
He has shown strength with his arm;
    he has scattered the proud in the thoughts of their hearts.
He has brought down the powerful from their thrones,
    and lifted up the lowly;
he has filled the hungry with good things,
    and sent the rich away empty.
He has helped his servant Israel,
    in remembrance of his mercy,
according to the promise he made to our ancestors,
    to Abraham and to his descendants for ever."

And Mary remained with her about three months and then returned to her home.

3. The Nativity

Matthew 1:18–2:12

Now the birth of Jesus the Messiah took place in this way. When his mother Mary had been engaged to Joseph, but before they lived together, she was found to be with child from the Holy Spirit. Her husband Joseph, being a righteous man and unwilling to expose her to public disgrace, planned to dismiss her quietly. But just when he had resolved to do this, an angel of the Lord appeared to him in a dream and said, "Joseph, son of David, do not be afraid to take Mary as your wife, for the child conceived in her is from the Holy Spirit. She will bear a son, and you are to name him Jesus, for he will save his people from their sins." All this took place to fulfill what had been spoken by the Lord through the prophet:

"Look, the virgin shall conceive
    and bear a son,
and they shall name him Emmanuel,"

which means, "God is with us."

When Joseph awoke from sleep, he did as the angel of the Lord commanded him; he took her as his wife, but had no marital relations with her until she had borne a son; and he named him Jesus.

In the time of King Herod, after Jesus was born in Bethlehem of Judæa, wise men from the East came to Jerusalem, asking, "Where is the child who has been born king of the Jews? For we observed his star at its rising, and have come to pay him homage." When King Herod heard this, he was frightened, and all Jerusalem with him; and calling together all the chief priests and scribes of the people, he inquired of them where the Messiah was to be born. They told him, "In Bethlehem of Judæa; for so it has been written by the prophet:
'And you, Bethlehem, in the land of Judah,
are by no means least among the rulers of Judah;
for from you shall come a ruler who is to shepherd my people Israel.' "
Then Herod secretly called for the wise men and learned from them the exact time when the star had appeared. Then he sent them to Bethlehem, saying, "Go and search diligently for the child; and when you have found him, bring me word so that I may also go and pay him homage." When they had heard the king, they set out; and there, ahead of them, went the star that they had seen at its rising, until it stopped over the place where the child was. When they saw that the star had stopped, they were overwhelmed with joy. On entering the house, they saw the child with Mary his mother; and they knelt down and paid him homage. Then, opening their treasure chests, they offered him gifts of gold, frankincense, and myrrh. And having been warned in a dream not to return to Herod, they left for their own country by another road.

Luke 2:1–20

In those days a decree went out from Emperor Augustus that all the world should be registered. This was the first registration and was taken while Quirinius was governor of Syria. All went to their own towns to be registered. Joseph also went from the town of Nazareth in Galilee to Judæa, to the city of David called Bethlehem, because he was descended from the house and family of David. He went to be registered with Mary, to whom he was engaged and who was expecting a child. While they were there, the time came for her to deliver her child. And she gave birth to her firstborn son and wrapped him in bands of cloth, and laid him in a manger, because there was no place for them in the inn.

In that region there were shepherds living in the fields, keeping watch over their flock by night. Then an angel of the Lord stood before them, and the glory of the Lord shone around them, and they were terrified. But the angel said to them, "Do not be afraid; for see—I am bringing you good news of great joy for all the people: to you is born this day in the city of David a Savior, who is the Messiah, the Lord. This will be a sign for you: you will find a child wrapped in bands of cloth and

lying in a manger." And suddenly there was with the angel a multitude of the heavenly host, praising God and saying,
"Glory to God in the highest heaven,
and on earth peace among those whom he favors!"

When the angels had left them and gone into heaven, the shepherds said one to another, "Let us go now to Bethlehem and see this thing that has taken place, which the Lord has made known to us." So they went with haste and found Mary and Joseph, and the child lying in the manger. When they saw this, they made known what had been told them about this child; and all who heard it were amazed at what the shepherds told them. But Mary treasured all these words and pondered them in her heart. The shepherds returned, glorifying and praising God for all they had heard and seen, as it had been told them.

4. The Presentation

Luke 2:22–35

When the time came for their purification according to the law of Moses, they brought him up to Jerusalem to present him to the Lord (as it is written in the law of the Lord, "Every firstborn male shall be designated as holy to the Lord"), and they offered a sacrifice according to what is stated in the law of the Lord, "a pair of turtledoves or two young pigeons."

Now there was a man in Jerusalem whose name was Simeon; this man was righteous and devout, looking forward to the consolation of Israel, and the Holy Spirit rested on him. It had been revealed to him by the Holy Spirit that he would not see death before he had seen the Lord's Messiah. Guided by the Spirit, Simeon came into the temple; and when the parents brought in the child Jesus, to do for him what was customary under the law, Simeon took him in his arms and praised God, saying,
"Master, now you are dismissing your servant in peace,
according to your word;
for my eyes have seen your salvation,
which you have prepared in the presence of all peoples,
a light for revelation to the Gentiles
and for glory to your people Israel."

And the child's father and mother were amazed at what was being said about him. Then Simeon blessed them and said to his mother Mary, "This child is destined for the falling and the rising of many in Israel, and to be a sign that will be opposed so that the thoughts of many will be revealed—and a sword will pierce your own soul too."

5. The Finding in the Temple

Luke 2:41–52

Now every year [Jesus'] parents went to Jerusalem for the festival of the Passover. And when he was twelve years old, they went up as usual for the festival. When the festival was ended and they started to return, the boy Jesus stayed behind in Jerusalem, but his parents did not know it. Assuming that he was in the group of travelers, they went a day's journey. Then they started to look for him among their relatives and friends. When they did not find him, they returned to Jerusalem to search for him. After three days they found him in the temple, sitting among the teachers, listening to them and asking them questions. And all who heard him were amazed at his understanding and his answers. When his parents saw him they were astonished; and his mother said to him, "Child, why have you treated us like this? Look, your father and I have searching for you in great anxiety." He said to them, "Why were you searching for me? Did you not know that I must be in my Father's house?" But they did not understand what he said to them. Then he went down with them and came to Nazareth, and was obedient to them. His mother treasured all these things in her heart.

And Jesus increased in wisdom and in years, and in divine and human favor.

The Luminous Mysteries

1. The Baptism of Jesus in the Jordan

Matthew 3:13–17

Then Jesus came from Galilee to John at the Jordan, to be baptized by him. John would have prevented him, saying, "I need to be baptized by you, and do you come to me?" But Jesus answered him, "Let it be so now; for it is proper for us in this way to fulfill all righteousness." Then he consented. And when Jesus had been baptized, just as he came up from the water, suddenly the heavens were opened to him and he saw the Spirit of God descending like a dove and alighting on him. And a voice from heaven said, "This is my Son, the Beloved, with whom I am well pleased."

(See also Mark 1:9–11, Luke 3:21–22, and John 1:29–34)

2. The Wedding at Cana

John 2:1–11

On the third day there was a wedding in Cana of Galilee, and the mother of Jesus was there. Jesus and his disciples had also been invited to the wedding. When the wine gave out, the mother of Jesus said to him, "They have no wine." And Jesus said to her, "Woman, what concern is that to you and to me? My hour has not yet come." His mother said to the servants, "Do whatever he tells you." Now standing there were six stone water jars for the Jewish rites of purification, each holding twenty or thirty gallons. Jesus said to them, "Fill the jars with water." And they filled them up to the brim. He said to them, "Now draw some out, and take it to the chief steward." So they took it. When the chief steward tasted the water that had become wine, and did not know where it came from (though the servants who had drawn the water knew), the steward called the bridegroom and said to him, "Everyone serves the good wine first, and then the inferior wine after the guests have become drunk. But you have kept the good wine until now." Jesus did this, the first of his signs, in Cana of Galilee, and revealed his glory; and his disciples believed in him.

3. THE PREACHING OF THE COMING OF THE KINGDOM OF GOD

A. Matthew 4:12–17, 23–25

Now when Jesus heard that John had been arrested, he withdrew to Galilee. He left Nazareth and made his home in Capernaum by the sea, in the territory of Zebulon and Naphthali, so that what had been spoken through the prophet Isaiah might be fulfilled:
"Land of Zebulon, land of Naphthali,
on the road by the sea, across the Jordan, Galilee of the Gentiles—
the people who sat in darkness have seen a great light,
and for those who sat in the region and shadow of death
light has dawned."
From that time Jesus began to proclaim, "Repent, for the kingdom of heaven has come near."

Jesus went throughout Galilee, teaching in their synagogues and proclaiming the good news of the kingdom and curing every disease and every sickness among the people. So his fame spread throughout all Syria, and they brought to him all the sick, those who were afflicted with various diseases and pains, demoniacs, epileptics, and paralytics, and he cured them. And great crowds followed him from Galilee, the Decapolis, Jerusalem, Judæa, and from beyond the Jordan.

(See also Mark 1:14–15 and Luke 4:14–21)

B. Luke 5:18–26

Just then some men came, carrying a paralyzed man on a bed. They were trying to bring him in and lay him before Jesus; but finding no way to bring him in because of the crowd, they went up on the roof and let him down with his bed through the tiles into the middle of the crowd in front of Jesus. When he saw their faith, he said, "Friend, your sins are forgiven you." Then the scribes and the Pharisees began to question, "Who is this who is speaking blasphemies? Who can forgive sins but God alone?" When Jesus perceived their questionings, he answered them, "Why do you raise such questions in your hearts? Which is easier, to say, 'Your sins are forgiven you,' or to say, 'Stand up and walk'? But so that you may know that the Son of Man has authority on earth to forgive sins"—he said to the one who was paralyzed—"I say to you, stand up and take your bed and go to your home." Immediately he stood up before them, took what he had been lying on, and went to his

home, glorifying God. Amazement seized all of them, and they glorified God and were filled with awe, saying, "We have seen strange things today."
(See also Matthew 9:2–8 and Mark 2:3–12)

C. *Luke* 7:36–50

One of the Pharisees asked Jesus to eat with him, and he went into the Pharisee's house and took his place at the table. And a woman in the city, who was a sinner, having learned that he was eating in the Pharisee's house, brought an alabaster jar of ointment. She stood behind him at his feet, weeping, and began to bathe his feet with her tears and to dry them with her hair. Then she continued kissing his feet and anointing them with the ointment. Now when the Pharisee who had invited him saw it, he said to himself, "If this man were a prophet, he would have known who and what kind of woman this is who is touching him—that she is a sinner." Jesus spoke up and said to him, "Simon, I have something to say to you." "Teacher," he replied, "speak." "A certain creditor had two debtors; one owed five hundred *denarii*, and the other fifty. When they could not pay, he canceled the debts for both of them. Now which of them will love him more?" Simon answered, "I suppose the one for whom he canceled the greater debt." And Jesus said to him, "You have judged rightly." Then turning toward the woman, he said to Simon, "Do you see this woman? I entered into your house; you gave me no water for my feet, but she has bathed my feet with her tears and dried them with her hair. You gave me no kiss, but from the time I came in she has not stopped kissing my feet. You did not anoint my head with oil, but she has anointed my feet with ointment. Therefore, I tell you, her sins, which were many, are forgiven; hence she has shown great love. But the one to whom little is forgiven, loves little." And he said to the woman, "Your sins are forgiven." But those who were at the table with him began to say among themselves, "Who is this who even forgives sins?" And he said to the woman, "Your faith has saved you; go in peace."
(See also Matthew 26:6–13, Mark 14:3–9, and John 12:1–8)

4. THE TRANSFIGURATION

Matthew 17:1–8

Jesus took with him Peter and James and his brother John and led them up a high mountain, by themselves. And he was transfigured before them, and his face shone like the sun, and his clothes became dazzling white. Suddenly there appeared to them Moses and Elijah, talking with him. Then Peter said to Jesus, "Lord, it is good for us to be here; if you wish, I will make three dwellings here, one for you, one for Moses, and one for Elijah." While he was still speaking, suddenly a bright cloud overshadowed them, and from the cloud a voice said, "This is my Son, the Beloved; with him I am well pleased; listen to him!" When the disciples heard this, they fell to the ground and were overcome by fear. But Jesus came and touched them, saying, "Get up and do be not afraid." And when they looked up, they saw no one except Jesus himself alone.

(See also Mark 9:2–8 and Luke 9:28–35)

5. THE INSTITUTION OF THE EUCHARIST

Mark 14:12–25

On the first day of Unleavened Bread, when the Passover lamb is sacrificed, his disciples said to him, "Where do you want us to go and make the preparations for you to eat the Passover?" So he sent two of his disciples, saying to them, "Go into the city, and a man carrying a jar of water will meet you; follow him, and wherever he enters, say to the owner of the house, 'The Teacher asks, Where is my guest room where I may eat the Passover with my disciples?' He will show you a large room upstairs, furnished and ready. Make preparations for us there." So the disciples set out and went to the city, and found everything as he had told them; and they prepared the Passover meal.

When it was evening, he came with the twelve. And when they had taken their places and were eating, Jesus said, "Truly I tell you, one of you will betray me, one who is eating with me." They began to be distressed and to say to him one after another, "Surely, not I?" He said to them, "It is one of the twelve, one who is dipping bread into the bowl with me. For the Son of Man goes as it is written of him, but woe to that one by whom the Son of Man is betrayed! It would have been better for that one not to have been born."

While they were eating, he took a loaf of bread, and after blessing it he broke it, gave it to them, and said, "Take; this is my body." Then he took a cup, and after giving thanks he gave it to them, and all of them drank from it. He said to them, "This is my blood of the covenant, which is poured out for many. Truly I tell you, I will never again drink of the fruit of the vine until that day when I drink it new in the kingdom of God."

I Corinthians 11:23–26

For I received from the Lord what I also handed on to you, that the Lord Jesus on the night when he was betrayed took a loaf of bread, and when he had given thanks, he broke it and said, "This is my body that is for you. Do this in remembrance of me." In the same way he took the cup also, after supper, saying, "This cup is the new covenant in my blood. Do this, as often as you drink it, in remembrance of me." For as often as you eat this bread and drink the cup, you proclaim the Lord's death until he comes.

(See also Matthew 26:17 – 29 and Luke 22:7–20)

The Sorrowful Mysteries

1. The Agony in The Garden

Mark 14:32–42

They went to a place called Gethsemane; and [Jesus] said to his disciples, "Sit here while I pray." He took with him Peter and James and John, and began to be distressed and agitated. And said to them, "I am deeply grieved, even to death; remain here, and keep awake." And going a little farther, he threw himself on the ground and prayed that, if it were possible, the hour might pass from him. He said, "*Abba*, Father, for you all things are possible; remove this cup from me; yet, not what I want, but what you want." He came and found them sleeping; and he said to Peter, "Simon, are you asleep? Could you not keep awake one hour? Keep awake and pray that you may not come into the time of trial; the spirit indeed is willing, but the flesh is weak." And again he went away and prayed, saying the same words. And once more he came and found them sleeping, for their eyes were very heavy; and they did not know what to say to him. He came a third time and said to them, "Are you still sleeping and taking your rest? Enough! The hour has come; the Son of Man is betrayed into the hands of sinners. Get up, let us be going. See, my betrayer is at hand."

(See also Matthew 26:36–46 and Luke 22:39–46)

2. The Scourging

Mark 15:6–15

Now at the festival [Pilate] used to release a prisoner for them, anyone for whom they asked. Now a man called Barabbas was in prison with the rebels who had committed murder during the insurrection. So the crowd came and began to ask Pilate to do for them according to his custom. Then he answered them, "Do you want me to release for you the King of the Jews?" For he realized that it was out of jealousy that the chief priests had handed him over. But the chief priests stirred up the crowd to have him release Barabbas for them instead. Pilate spoke to them again, "Then what do you wish me to do with the man you call the King of the Jews?" They shouted back, "Crucify him!" Pilate asked them, "Why, what evil has he done?" But they shouted all the more, "Crucify him!" So Pilate, wishing to satisfy the crowd, released Barabbas for them; and after flogging Jesus, he handed him over to be crucified.

(See also Matthew 27:15–26, Luke 23:13–24, and John 18:38b–19:1)

3. The Crowning with Thorns

Matthew 27:27–31a

Then the soldiers of the governor took Jesus into the governor's headquarters, and they gathered the whole cohort around him. They stripped him and put a scarlet robe on him, and after twisting some thorns into a crown, they put it on his head. They put a reed in his right hand and knelt before him and mocked him, saying, "Hail, King of the Jews!" They spat on him, and took the reed and struck him on the head. After mocking him, they stripped him of the robe and put his own clothes on him.

Mark 15:16–20*a*

Then the soldiers led him into the courtyard of the palace (that is, the governor's headquarters); and they called together the whole cohort. And they clothed him in a purple cloak; and after twisting some thorns into a crown, they put it on him. And they began saluting him, "Hail, King of the Jews!" They struck his head with a reed, spat upon him, and knelt down in homage to him. After mocking him, they stripped him of the purple cloak and put his own clothes on him.

(See also John 19:2–3*)*

4. THE BEARING OF THE CROSS

Mark 15:20*b*–21

Then they led [Jesus] out to crucify him. They compelled a passer-by, who was coming in from the country, to carry his cross; it was Simon of Cyrene, the father of Alexander and Rufus.

Luke 23:26–32

As they led [Jesus] away, they seized a man, Simon of Cyrene, who was coming from the country, and they laid the cross on him, and made him carry it behind Jesus. A great number of the people followed him, and among them were women who were beating their breasts and wailing for him. But Jesus turned to them and said, "Daughters of Jerusalem, do not weep for me, but weep for yourselves and for your children. For the days are surely coming when they will say, 'Blessed are the barren, and the wombs that never bore, and the breasts that never nursed.' Then they will begin to say to the mountains, 'Fall on us;' and to the hills, 'Cover us.' For if they do this when the wood is green, what will happen when it is dry?"

Two others also, who were criminals, were led away to be put to death with him.

(See also Matthew 27:31*b*–32 *and John* 19:16–17*)*

5. THE CRUCIFIXION

Mark 15:22–37

Then they brought Jesus to the place called Golgotha (which means the place of a skull). And they offered him wine mixed with myrrh; but he did not take it. And they crucified him, and divided his clothes among them, casting lots to decide what each should take.

It was nine o'clock in the morning when they crucified him. The inscription of the charge against him read, "The King of the Jews." And with him they crucified two bandits, one on his right and one on his left. Those who passed by derided him, shaking their heads and saying, "Aha! You who would destroy the temple and build it in three days, save yourself, and come down from the cross!" In the same way the chief priests, along with the scribes, were also mocking him among themselves and saying, "He saved others; he cannot save himself. Let the Messiah, the King of Israel, come down from the cross now, so that we may see and believe." Those who were crucified with him also taunted him.

When it was noon, darkness came over the whole land until three in the afternoon. At three o'clock Jesus cried out with a loud voice, *"Eloi, Eloi, lema sabachthani?"* which means, "My God, my God, why have you forsaken me?" When some of the bystanders heard it, they said, "Listen, he is calling for Elijah." And someone ran, filled a sponge with sour wine, put it on a stick, and gave it to him to drink, saying, "Wait, let us see whether Elijah will come to take him down." Then Jesus gave a loud cry and breathed his last.

John 19:18–30

There they crucified him, and with him two others, one on either side, with Jesus between them. Pilate also had an inscription written and put on the cross. It read, "Jesus of Nazareth, the King of the Jews." Many of the Jews read this inscription, because the place where Jesus was crucified was near the city; and it was written in Hebrew, in Latin, and in Greek. Then the chief priests of the Jews said to Pilate, "Do not write, 'The King of the Jews,' but, 'This man said, I am King of the Jews.' " Pilate answered, "What I have written I have written." When the soldiers had crucified Jesus, they took his clothes and divided them into four parts, one for each soldier. They also took his tunic; now the tunic was seamless, woven in one piece from the top. So they said to one another, "Let us not tear it, but cast lots for it to see who will get it." This was to fulfill what the scripture says,

"They divided my clothes among themselves,
and for my clothing they cast lots."

And that is what the soldiers did.

Meanwhile, standing near the cross of Jesus were his mother, and his mother's sister, Mary the wife of Clopas, and Mary Magdalene. When Jesus saw his mother and the disciple whom he loved standing beside her, he said to his mother, "Woman, here is your son." Then he said to the disciple, "Here is your mother." And from that hour the disciple took her into his own home.

After this, when Jesus knew that all was now finished, he said (in order to fulfill the scripture), "I am thirsty." A jar full of sour wine was standing there. So they put a sponge full of the wine on a branch of hyssop and held it to his mouth. When Jesus had received the wine, he said, "It is finished." Then he bowed his head and gave up his spirit.

(See also Matthew 27:33–50 and Luke 23:33–46)

The Glorious Mysteries

1. The Resurrection

Matthew 28:1–10

After the sabbath, as the first day of the week was dawning, Mary Magdalene and the other Mary went to see the tomb. And suddenly there was a great earthquake; for an angel of the Lord, descending from heaven, came and rolled back the stone and sat on it. His appearance was like lightning, and his clothing white as snow. For fear of him the guards shook and became like dead men. But the angel said to the women, "Do not be afraid; I know that you are looking for Jesus who was crucified. He is not here; for he has been raised, as he said. Come, see the place where he lay. Then go quickly and tell his disciples, 'He has been raised from the dead, and indeed he is going ahead of you to Galilee; there you will see him.' This is my message for you." So they left the tomb quickly with fear and great joy, and ran to tell his disciples. Suddenly Jesus met them and said, "Greetings!" And they came to him, took hold of his feet, and worshiped him. Then Jesus said to them, "Do not be afraid; go and tell my brothers to go to Galilee; there they will see me."

Mark 16:1–8

When the sabbath was over, Mary Magdalene, and Mary the mother of James, and Salome bought spices, so that they might go and anoint him. And very early on the first day of the week, when the sun had risen, they went to the tomb. They had been saying to one another, "Who will roll away the stone for us from the entrance to the tomb?" When they looked up, they saw that the stone, which was very large, had already been rolled back. As they entered the tomb, they saw a young man, dressed in a white robe, sitting on the right side; and they were alarmed. But he said to them, "Do not be alarmed; you are looking for Jesus of Nazareth, who was crucified. He has been raised; he is not here. Look, there is the place they laid him. But go, tell his disciples and Peter that he is going ahead of you to Galilee; there you will see him, just as he told you." So they went out and fled from the tomb, for terror and amazement had seized them; and they said nothing to anyone, for they were afraid.

Luke 24:1–12

But on the first day of the week, at early dawn, they came to the tomb, taking the spices that they had prepared. They found the stone rolled away from the tomb, but when they went in, they did not find the body. While they were perplexed about this, suddenly two men in dazzling clothes stood beside them. The women were terrified and bowed their faces to the ground, but the men said to them, "Why do you look for the living among the dead? He is not here, but has risen. Remember how he told you, while he was still in Galilee, that the Son of Man must be handed over to sinners, and be crucified, and on the third day rise again." Then they remembered his words, and returning from the tomb, they told all this to the eleven and to all the rest. Now it was Mary Magdalene, Joanna, Mary the mother of James, and the other women with them who told this to the apostles. But these words seemed to them an idle tale, and they did not believe them. But Peter got up and ran to the tomb; stooping and looking in, he saw the linen cloths by themselves; then he went home, amazed at what had happened.

John 20:1–18

Early on the first day of the week, while it was still dark, Mary Magdalene came to the tomb and saw that the stone had been removed from the tomb. So she ran and went to Simon Peter and the other disciple, the one whom Jesus loved, and said to them, "They have taken the Lord out of the tomb, and we do not know where they have laid him." Then Peter and the other disciple set out and went toward the tomb. The two were running together, but the other disciple outran Peter and reached the tomb first. He bent down to look in and saw the linen wrappings lying there, but he did not go in. Then Simon Peter came, following him, and went into the tomb. He saw the linen wrappings lying there, and the cloth that had been on Jesus' head, not lying with the linen wrappings but rolled up in a place by itself. Then the other disciple, who reached the tomb first, also went in, and he saw and believed; for as yet they did not understand the scripture, that he must rise from the dead. Then the disciples returned to their homes.

But Mary stood weeping outside the tomb. As she wept, she bent over to look into the tomb; and she saw two angels in white, sitting where the body of Jesus had been lying, one at the head and the other at the feet. They said to her, "Woman, why are you weeping?" She said to them, "They have taken away my Lord, and I do not know where they have laid him." When she had said this, she turned around and saw Jesus standing there, but she did not know that it was Jesus. Jesus said to her, "Woman, why are you weeping? Whom are you looking for?" Supposing him to be the gardener, she said to him, "Sir, if you have carried him away, tell me where you have laid him, and I will take him away." Jesus said to her, "Mary!" She turned and said to him in Hebrew, *"Rabbouni!"* (which means Teacher). Jesus said to her, "Do not hold on to me, because I have not yet ascended to the Father. But go to my brothers and say to them, 'I am ascending to my Father and your Father, to my God and your God.'" Mary Magdalene went and announced to the disciples, "I have seen the Lord;" and she told them that he had said these things to her.

2. THE ASCENSION

Mark 16:19–20

So then the Lord Jesus, after he had spoken to them, was taken up into heaven and sat down at the right hand of God. And they went out and proclaimed the good news everywhere, while the Lord worked with them and confirmed the message by the signs that accompanied it.

Luke 24:50–53

Then [Jesus] led [the eleven and their companions] out as far as Bethany, and, lifting up his hands, he blessed them. While he was blessing them, he withdrew from them and was carried up into heaven. And they worshiped him, and returned to Jerusalem with great joy; and they were continually in the temple blessing God.

Acts 1:6–11

So when [the apostles] had come together, they asked [Jesus], "Lord, is this the time when you will restore the kingdom to Israel?" He replied, "It is not for you to know the times or periods that the Father has set by his own authority. But you will receive power when the Holy Spirit has come upon you; and you will be my witnesses in Jerusalem, in all Judæa and Samaria, and to the ends of the earth." When he had said this, as they were watching, he was lifted up, and a cloud took him out of their sight. While he was going and they were gazing up toward heaven, suddenly two men in white robes stood by them. They said, "Men of Galilee, why do you stand looking up toward heaven? This Jesus, who has been taken up from you into heaven, will come in the same way as you saw him go into heaven."

3. THE COMING OF THE HOLY SPIRIT AT PENTECOST

Acts 2:1–4

When the day of Pentecost had come, they were all together in one place. And suddenly from heaven there came a sound like the rush of a violent wind, and it filled the entire house where they were sitting. Divided tongues, as of fire, appeared among them, and a tongue rested on each of them. All of them were filled with the Holy Spirit and began to speak in other languages, as the Spirit gave them ability.

4. THE ASSUMPTION OF THE VIRGIN MARY

Revelation 12:1

A great portent appeared in heaven: a woman clothed with the sun, with the moon under her feet, and on her head a crown of twelve stars.

5. THE CORONATION OF THE VIRGIN MARY

II Timothy 4:8

From now on there is reserved for me the crown of righteousness, which the Lord, the righteous judge, will give me on that day, and not only to me but also to all who have longed for his appearing.

www.ingramcontent.com/pod-product-compliance
Lightning Source LLC
Chambersburg PA
CBHW052038070526
44584CB00020B/3158